The Way of Peace

J.C. Wenger

WIPF & STOCK · Eugene, Oregon

Wipf and Stock Publishers
199 W 8th Ave, Suite 3
Eugene, OR 97401

The Way of Peace
By Wenger, John C.

ISBN 13: 978-1-60608-953-8
Publication date 7/16/2009
Previously published by Herald Press, 1977

CONTENTS

PREFACE

Followers of Jesus Christ can be found today all over the world. Among these Christians are Mennonites who take their name from Menno Simons, a Frisian Reformer of the sixteenth century.

Until the nineteenth century, most Mennonites were found in Europe and North America. During the twentieth century, however, mission, relief, and service activities have resulted in a worldwide Mennonite fellowship.

One major emphasis of the Mennonites is to practice daily Christ's teaching to "love your enemies." This book outlines what it means to live this kind of life.

The Way of Peace is volume four of the Mennonite Faith Series listed inside the back cover. We hope the material will be of interest to anyone wanting to understand the Christian faith in general and Mennonites in particular.

Anyone wanting to study Mennonite faith and life further may check the references placed at the back of each book.

J. Allen Brubaker

1

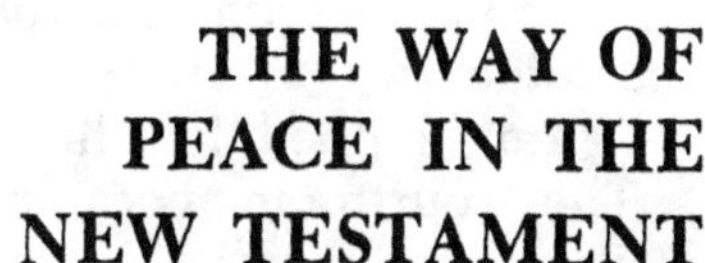

THE WAY OF PEACE IN THE NEW TESTAMENT

WHEN Jesus told His disciples how men would recognize them as His disciples—as children of God—He said, "By this all men will know that you are my disciples, if you have love for one another." He also said: "Love your enemies."

Christians of all times and places have displayed love and caring. It is their badge. Some have believed love and peace to be the Christian way of life in war as well as peace. They would not defend themselves against murder, rape, and looting, but choose rather "to turn the other cheek, to go the second mile," as Jesus said in His Sermon on the Mount.

Forgiving Love, Not Revenge

In Korea a generation ago, the only son of a Christian father was killed by a wicked youth. The guilty youth was arrested, tried, and found guilty. The judge was about to pronounce a dreadful sentence. At that point the Christian father of the dead youth stood up and asked permission to speak. His request was granted.

The father said: "I now no longer have a son. Instead of putting the youth who destroyed my son to death or into prison, I respectfully request this court to allow me to adopt him as my son—in place of the one I lost."

"Are you certain that you mean that?" asked the judge.

"I am," replied the Christian father.

The courtroom became quiet as everyone waited for the verdict.

"Granted," said the judge.

The story of the Christian father's amazing forgiveness, of returning good for evil, spread over Korea like wildfire. The Koreans named that place, "The City of Atomic Love."

Only God knows how much that father's act advanced the cause of Christ in that great land.

During World War II, Herr Mayr, a Catholic who believed in the way of peace for Christians, lived in Vienna, Austria. In the closing weeks of the war the Russian army, drunk with victory, was slowly passing through the city—looting, raping, destroying. One day Mayr looked out the front window and saw some soldiers turning into his walk. He quickly said to his nineteen-year-old daughter, "Go to the basement!"

The father then threw open the front door, and smiling, invited his visitors to come in. He then motioned them to be seated. Then he called his wife and children, including the grown daughter, into the room, and with gestures made it clear that this was his family. The mother then hastened to bring cake and coffee, and to feed the visitors as honored guests.

The soldiers were so amazed by this treatment that after the refreshments they quietly left. No rape. No murder. *Why?* It was not by might nor by power that the Christian father operated; it was by the omnipotent Spirit of God (see Zechariah 4:6).

Christ Taught Love and Forgiveness

When we turn again to the Scriptures we find other teachings of Jesus about the way of peace. Surely no one has suffered so much injustice, misunderstanding, and cruelty as Jesus suffered at the hands of His opposers. We see how He demonstrated love in action. Jesus said: "You have heard that it was said, 'An eye for an eye and a tooth for a tooth' [Exodus 21:24]. But I say to you, Do not resist one who is evil. But if any one strikes you on the right cheek, turn to him the other also" (Matthew 5:38, 39). Nonresistance of evildoers is based on this Scripture. Similarly, we are taught to overcome evil with good (Romans 12:21).

Compare the Lord's words in Luke 6:29, TEV: "If anyone hits you on one cheek, let him hit the other one too; if someone takes your coat, let him have your shirt as well."

Jesus taught: "You have heard that it was said, 'You shall love your neighbor and hate your enemy.' But I say to you, Love your enemies and pray for those who persecute you, so that you may be sons of your Father who is in heaven; for he makes his sun rise on the evil and on the good, and sends rain on the just and on the unjust" (Matthew 5:43-45).

Christ Lived Love and Forgiveness

When the Roman governor asked Jesus whether or not he was a king, our Lord replied: "My kingship is not of this world; if my kingship were of this world, my servants would fight, that I might not be handed over to the Jews; but my kingship is not from the world" (John 18:36).

The New Testament has these positive words: "Our citizenship is in heaven. And we eagerly await a Savior from there, the Lord Jesus Christ" (Philippians 3:20, NIV).

When Christ stood on trial for His life before Governor Pilate, He displayed remarkable poise and patience: "When he was accused by the chief priests and elders, he made no answer. Then Pilate said to him, 'Do you not hear how many things they testify against you?' But he gave him no answer, not even to a single charge; so that the governor wondered greatly" (Matthew 27:12-14).

The trial went against Him, and He was severely beaten and led out to be crucified: "And when they came to the place which is called The Skull, there they crucified him" (Luke 23:33).

Jesus could have summoned "twelve legions of

angels" to His defense (Matthew 26:53). Yet, He went to the death, saying, "Not my will, but thine be done" and "Forgive them; for they know not what they do" (Luke 22:42; 23:34).

Stephen Lived Peace

The Holy Spirit put this same spirit into the early believers, as we learn in the story of Stephen, the first Christian to die for his beliefs.

Luke writes of Stephen's testimony to his enemies in Acts 7:54-60. "When they heard these things they were enraged, and they ground their teeth against him. But he, full of the Holy Spirit, gazed into heaven and saw the glory of God, and Jesus standing at the right hand of God; and he said, 'Behold, I see the heavens opened, and the Son of man standing at the right hand of God.'

But they cried out with a loud voice and stopped their ears and rushed together upon him. Then they cast him out of the city and stoned him; and . . . he prayed, 'Lord Jesus, receive my spirit.' And he knelt down and cried with a loud voice, 'Lord, do not hold this sin against them!' And when he had said this, he fell asleep [in death]."

As we would expect, we find these same teachings in the writings of the apostles.

The Apostle Taught the Way of Peace

The Apostle Peter wrote: "You must all have the same attitude and the same feelings; love one another as brothers, and be kind and humble with one another. Do not pay back evil with evil, or cursing with cursing; instead pay back with a blessing, because a blessing is what God promised to give you when he called you" (1 Peter 3:8, 9, TEV).

And the Apostle Paul adds: "See that no one pays back wrong for wrong, but at all times make it your aim to do good to one another and to all people" (1 Thessalonians 5:15, TEV). "The Lord's servant must not quarrel; instead he must be kind to everyone" (2 Timothy 2:24, NIV).

Christ also suffered for us, writes Peter, leaving us an example, that we should follow His steps: "He committed no sin, and no one ever heard a lie come from his lips. When he was insulted, he did not answer back with an insult; when he suffered, he did not threaten, but placed his hopes in God, the righteous Judge" (1 Peter 2:22, 23, TEV). "Since Christ suffered physically you too must strengthen yourselves with the same way of thinking" (1 Peter 4:1, TEV).

Love Is the Power for Peace

The Apostle Paul wrote to the Romans in days of great persecution: "Do everything possible on your part to live in peace with everybody. Never take revenge, my friends, but instead let God's anger do it. For the Scripture says, 'I will take revenge, I will pay back, says the Lord.' Instead, as the Scripture says: 'If your enemy is hungry, feed him; if he is thirsty, give him a drink; for by doing this you will make him burn with shame.' Do not let evil defeat you; instead, conquer evil with good" (Romans 12:17-21, TEV).

Paul tells where the Christian gets power to

conquer evil. It is true that we live in the world, but we do not fight from worldly motives. The weapons we use in our fight are not the world's weapons, but God's powerful weapons, with which to destroy strongholds (2 Corinthians 10:3).

One of God's weapons is love. His love is the power that enables us to live the way of peace. John, whom Jesus had named "Son of Thunder,"was changed from a fighter to a man of love. We think of him as the "Beloved Disciple." His letters, written at the end of a long life, almost seem to breathe love. Listen to what he has to say about love. "Whoever loves his brother lives in the light" (1 John 2:10, TEV).

"We know that we have passed out of death into life, because we love the brethren. He who does not love abides in death" (1 John 3:14).

"Dear friends, let us love one another, because love comes from God. Whoever loves is a child of God and knows God" (1 John 4:7, TEV).

"He who does not love does not know God, for God is love" (1 John 4:8, TEV).

"God is love. Whoever lives in love lives in God, and God in him" (1 John 4:16, NIV).

"If any one says, 'I love God,' and hates his brother, he is a liar" (1 John 4:20).

These verses from John's letter can help us determine if we have Christ's empowering love. His forgiving love is the foundation for the way of peace in the New Testament—and in our time.

2

THE WAY OF PEACE THROUGH THE CENTURIES

OUTSTANDING church leaders in the early centuries of the Christian church have left on record their teachings and have reported the stand of the Christians of their days.

By looking at some of their statements we can trace Christian action for the first four centuries after Christ.

Statements from Early Church Leaders

Ignatius (AD 50-115), Bishop of Antioch and martyr, taught that Christians should not seek revenge on those who injure them. . . . Rather, we are to imitate the Lord, who when He was reviled, did not use abusive language; when He was crucified, He answered not; when He suffered, He threatened not, but prayed for His enemies.

Polycarp (AD 69-155), Bishop of Smyrna and martyr, instructed Christians to follow Christ, not returning evil for evil, nor scolding for scolding.

Justin Martyr (AD 100-165), Christian apologist and martyr, taught that we who were filled with war—have changed our warlike weapons—our swords into plowshares and our spears into farming implements (compare Isaiah 2:4; Micah 4:3).

Athenagoras (AD 150-200) said that we have learned not only not to return blow for blow, nor to go to law with those who plunder and rob us; but to those who smite us on the one side of the face we offer the other side also, and to those who take away our coat we give likewise our cloak.

Tertullian (AD 160-225), a lawyer and a Christian from 190, thought Christians should not take part in warfare when the Lord proclaims that he who uses the sword shall perish by the sword. Tertullian insisted that if a soldier becomes a Christian believer, he must leave the army at once.

Origen (AD 185-254) was a brilliant writer and teacher of Alexandria, Egypt. One of his best statements about taking part in warfare was written during the last decade of his life. In reply to Celsus, a pagan who opposed Christianity and Judaism, Origen wrote:

"We have come in accordance with the counsels of Jesus to cut down our warlike and arrogant swords of argument into ploughshares, and we convert into sickles the spears we formerly used in fighting. For we no longer take sword against nation, nor do we learn any more to make war, having become sons of peace for the sake of Jesus. (See volume IV of *Ante-Nicene Fathers,* Erdmans edition, 1965, pages 395-669, for full details of Origen's reply.)

Origen patiently takes up endless points of criticism made by Celsus against the Christians, and brilliantly replies to them. For example, Origen notes the necessary ethical differences between the Old Testament era and the Christian church of his day. He points out that Christians could not slay their enemies or condemn them to be burned or stoned as Moses did (*Against Celsus,* VII, 26).

In another context, Origen referred to the way Celsus belittled the nonresistant teaching of Jesus (turning the other cheek, and surrendering the cloak as well as the coat). He then proceeded to show the superiority of Jesus as an ethical Teacher over Plato (VII, 71). Origen was also aware of the sacredness of human life and therefore opposed any form of infanticide: God would have us bring up our children and not destroy any of the offspring given us by His providence (VIII, 55).

Christians Help by Their Prayers

Concerning warfare, Celsus had urged the Christians to assist the emperor with all their might and to labor with him in the maintenance of justice, that is, they were to fight under him or to lead an army along with him (VIII, 73).

Origen replied that we do indeed give the emperor help; but we give divine help! We put on the whole armor of God. We obey the command: I advise therefore that first of all humble requests, prayers, petitions, and giving of thanks, be made for all men; for kings and for all that are in authority. And the more anyone excels in piety, declared Origen, the more effective help does he give . . . even more than is given by soldiers who go forth to fight and kill as many of the enemy as they can!

Christians Live Peace

Origen declares that we do take our part in public affairs. Along with righteous prayers, we join self-denying exercises and meditations, which teach us to despise (worldly) pleasures, and not to be led away by them.

Origen continues: None fight better for the king (emperor) than we do. We do not indeed fight under him: but we fight on his behalf, forming a special army—an army of piety—by offering our prayers to God (VIII, 73).

Origen finally becomes bold: Christians benefit their country more than others. For they train up citizens and teach piety to the Supreme Being. They promote to a divine and heavenly city those whose lives in the smallest cities have been good and worthy (VIII, 74).

Celsus thought that Christians ought to accept office in the government of the country—which they, obviously, were not then doing.

Origen disagrees: Christians do not decline public office to escape public duties, but that they may reserve themselves for a diviner and more necessary service in the church of God—the salvation of men.

Maximilian Does Not Fear Death

In AD 295 a youth named Maximilian stood before a military commander in North Africa for induction into the Roman Army. Maximilian was a Christian who accepted Christ's teachings.

"I cannot serve as a soldier," declared Maximilian, "I cannot do evil. I am a Christian."

Christians had been saying that for many generations. So the commander put all the pressure on him that he could.

"Put on the uniform," he said, "or it will cost you your life!"

Maximilian was not to be frightened. Even the thought of execution did not move him. He knew His Lord, and he had no fear of death. Beyond death he would be with Christ!

"I shall not perish," he told the commander, "but when I have forsaken this world, my soul shall live with Christ my Lord."

Young Maximilian, only twenty-one, was executed for civil disobedience because he dared to stand for the beliefs the Christian church had always taught.

Killing of Christians Halted

A mighty military man, Constantine was in a campaign in England in 306 when his father, the Western emperor, proclaimed him his successor at York. The full name of this emperor (AD 306-337) was Flavius Valerius Aurelius Constantinus. In 313 Constantine forbade any further persecution of the Christians. In 323 he made Byzantium his capital, and named it after himself, Constantinople, (now Istanbul). He convened and chaired the great Council of Nicea, though not a baptized member himself! Constantine bestowed many favors on the church. He made it possible for people to make bequests to the church; he granted the clergy exemption from military service, made the observance of the Lord's day an Imperial regulation, and contributed liberally to the building of houses of worship for the Christians. During all of this he remained a heathen high priest, at least in name, all his life and his coins still bore heathen emblems. He did, however, finally receive baptism on his deathbed.

Churchmen Justify War

It is unbelievable how the Christians scrambled to show their gratitude to this great emperor who so amazingly favored the church. It does not seem possible that the leaders of the Christian church could so rapidly reverse themselves on such a basic matter as military service and warfare. But the record is clear: even the top leaders hastened to assert that Christians could now take life in wartime.

Athanasius (AD 196-372), Bishop of Alexandria, renowned defender of orthodoxy, and metropolitan (chief bishop) of all Egypt and

Libya, had the courage to stand for the truth as he saw it. He was banished four times by the Roman emperors and spent no less than twenty years in exile. He dared to stand against the whole world, and the phrase "Anthanasius against the world" became a well-known testimony to his courage. Yet on the matter of nonresistance, he too crumpled and bowed the knee to the empire. He held firmly to the principle that human life was sacred, and that personal killing was a sin. "But to kill one's adversary in war is both lawful and praiseworthy."

Ambrose (AD 340-397), Bishop of Milan, Italy, had been a popular magistrate. At age 34 he was not yet a member of the church; however, he was receiving instruction in the Christian faith in preparation for baptism. When he appeared at the church following the death of the previous bishop, the people began to shout, "Ambrose for bishop!" Although he had actually gone to the church to keep civil order, he suddenly found himself chosen bishop. It took only eight days to get him baptized and to bring him up through the intermediate steps prior to his being consecrated a bishop! That was in 374. For twenty-three years this gifted scholar, preacher, and orator served as bishop of Milan. The Ambrosian Chant is named for him. He won the respect of the pagan Augustine, and when he was converted, baptized him.

On the subject of nonresistance, Ambrose also praised soldiers who fight for their homeland. Such courage, he said, is "full of righteousness."

Augustine (AD 354-430), Bishop of Hippo in North Africa, is acknowledged universally to have been the most influential of all the leaders of the ancient church. Converted at 32, he became a priest in 391, and a bishop four years later. For the next twenty-five years he was the most influential voice in Christendom. Preacher, bishop, writer, defender of the faith, and theologian, he exerted enormous influence everywhere. To his great dismay he saw Rome captured and looted by the Germanic Visigoths in 410. He was deeply shaken, and profoundly concerned that civilization should not collapse. (However, the Western Roman Empire fell in 476, in spite of efforts to save it.) Perhaps this contributed to the vigor with which he declared that it was right for Christians to serve in the military. It was Bishop Augustine who proposed and developed the concept that some wars are "just." This concept has soothed the consciences of Christians on both sides of every war since his time!

Christ taught His disciples that they should be ready to suffer injury and death but not to defend themselves. However, this New Testament teaching was largely forgotten after Augustine led the church to believe that its members could participate in a "just war." Catholic orders of monks and nuns were of course expected to follow the New Testament teaching, but the remainder of the church could follow the lower standards the church had accepted. The Roman Empire had both Eastern and Western Emperors after 364. In 380, by joint edict, the Eastern Theodosius and the Western Gratian made

Roman Catholicism the official religion of state. In 416, just six years after Rome was sacked, the empire required all soldiers to be at least Christian in name!

As we have seen, nonresistance was the position of all leaders and writers in the ancient Christian church until the time of Constantine the Great. But the greatest churchman of the early fifth century, the mighty Augustine, introduced and taught the doctrine of the so-called "Just War." Unfortunately, this has become the general position of the larger part of the Christian church since that time.

The Reformers Rediscover the Way of Peace

For the next eight centuries after Constantine and Augustine, the lamp of the church burned low. These were the Dark Ages.

About AD 1200 flickering lights of renewal began to appear in Europe. We speak of this broadly as the Age of Reformation.

Waldo. A Reformer of South France, Waldo by name, lived about 1140 to 1217. He was mightily used of God to restore New Testament Christianity widely on the continent of Europe. He wanted Christians to follow faithfully the stern demands of the New Testament. One of his emphases was nonresistance—refusing to use force to conquer one's enemies. In the centuries following Waldo's death, the Catholic Church made vigorous efforts to wipe out his "heresy." During this period, the Waldenses failed to retain Waldo's teaching on Christ's way of peace.

Chelcicky. Likewise, the fifteenth-century

radical Czech Reformer, Peter Chelcicky, was a firm adherent of New Testament nonresistance. In the course of time, however, the light he sought to kindle was allowed to flicker and finally go out also.

Luther. In 1520 when Luther was carrying on a mighty campaign to bring renewal to the Roman Catholic Church, he did not hesitate to put Dr. John Eck in his place:

> You say that I would give room to the peace-breakers and murderers because I have taught that a Christian should abstain from violence and should not fight to recover his belongings of which he was robbed. Why do you not rebuke Christ who has taught this?

In the end, however, Luther became frightened and set aside his belief in nonresistance. He then urged the German princes to crush the local peasant revolt ruthlessly.

Zwingli, the great Swiss Reformer, hated war with all his heart. He had accompanied Swiss mercenaries as their chaplain, and was sick of war. In the years after that experience, he often spoke out as if he were a nonresistant. For example, in 1522:

> Considered from the Christian point of view it is by no means right to have a part in war. According to Christ's teaching we should pray for those who despitefully use us and persecute us, and if an aggressor smites us on the right cheek (we should) turn to him the other also.

Although Zwingli hated war, opposed war, and even talked like a pacifist at times, in the end he joined the military forces of Zurich and fell in the Battle of Cappel, 1531.

Calvin. John Calvin, the Reformed leader of Geneva, Switzerland, says concerning Christ's teaching in Matthew 5:45.

> When he expressly declares that no one man will be a child of God unless he *love those who hate him*, who shall dare to say that we are not bound to observe this doctrine? The statement amounts to this, "Whoever shall wish to be accounted a Christian, let him *love his enemies*." It is truly horrible and monstrous that the world should have been covered with such thick darkness for three or four centuries as not to see that it is an express command, and that everyone who neglects it is struck out of the number of the children of God.

Three cheers for Calvin! Who could say it better? Yet when he became a part of the religious government of Geneva, Calvin decided it was his duty to drive the heretics out of the world! This applied to Servetus and to a number of others.

Zwingli, Calvin, and others after them took a "practical" course of action when they felt the evangelical cause in danger. They decided to accompany the troops to defend the gospel with the sword. This compromise still remains a danger for the Christian church today.

The Anabaptists

From the Reformation in Switzerland arose a

group to become known as Anabaptist (re-baptizers) of which the first leaders were Grebel, Mantz, Blaurock, and others. These embraced and promoted the doctrine of nonresistance.

Conrad Grebel. Zwingli's one-time disciple, Conrad Grebel, had become a firm believer in the doctrine of absolute love and nonresistance. He wrote a letter on September 5, 1524, setting forth his ideas. In this well thought-out epistle to the German Reformer Muentzer, Grebel asserts that the gospel and its adherents are not to be protected by the sword—nor shall the adherents defend themselves. True, believing sheep, said Grebel and his brethren, are "sheep among wolves, sheep for the slaughter." Christians, asserted Grebel, "must be baptized in anxiety, distress, affliction, persecution, suffering, and death. They must pass through the test of fire, and reach the Fatherland of eternal rest, not by slaying their bodily enemies but their spiritual enemies." Grebel was crystal clear in his conviction that the Christian ethic does not permit Christians to go to war. "They employ neither worldly sword nor war, since with them killing is absolutely renounced."

Grebel's conviction was shared deeply by his colleague, Felix Mantz, who openly opposed capital punishment and was drowned for his faith in January 1527. The leading theologian of the Swiss and South German Anabaptism of the Zurich variety, Michael Sattler, was equally dedicated to the theology of the suffering church and to the ethic of nonresistance. All these believers saw the ethic of the Christian set forth in the life and teaching of the Prince of Peace, Jesus Christ our Lord.

Dirk and Obbe. Not all Dutch Mennonites accepted the nonresistance doctrine. One group of Anabaptists in Netherlands, however, was led by such biblicists as Obbe Philips and his brother Dirk. This group was strongly nonresistant from the start. Menno Simons, a gifted Catholic priest who had united with "Obbenites" in 1536, was ordained as an elder (bishop) by Obbe in 1537. Later Obbe became discouraged and withdrew from the movement by 1540. For twenty-five years Menno and Dirk continued to guide the peaceful Anabaptists of the Low Countries and of North Germany by their ministry of the Word and by their writings.

Simons. Menno Simons was the most influential sixteenth-century Anabaptist. His writings, particularly the *Foundation* book, provided doctrinal and ethical guidance to the Mennonites through the centuries. Menno opposed both war and the killing of criminals.

The most distinct teaching of the Anabaptists was absolute love. This doctrine came to be called "nonresistance"—no resistance to force. The Anabaptists expressed this teaching with a word which means the "doctrine of being unarmed," of not defending oneself or others. Christians who accept this way of peace would rather be wronged than do wrong to someone else; they would rather die than kill, even in self-defense or in warfare. Or, from another point of view, Christians who follow the way of peace place themselves in God's care. They are committed in advance to bear whatever He may allow to come upon them. Mennonites (named for Menno Simons) accept the Anabaptist teaching of nonresistance.

The Church Today

There are individual Christians in all the major denominations who hold the peace position. Only three small denominations are classed as Historic Peace Churches: the Mennonites, the Church of the Brethren (called German Baptists prior to 1908), and the Society of Friends (Quakers). A few small groups around the globe consider themselves peace churches, but many Christians have never heard of the doctrine. Many persons are surprised when they first hear about the way of peace. It seems to them an unbelievable doctrine. Their first reaction is that such a strong position is contrary to all reason. "What would you do if. . . ?" they ask. Most Christians are not eager to give serious consideration to absolute nonresistance! People refuse to look seriously at the teaching of the New Testament on "the royal law" of love, for it is a costly way (James 2:8). "Does not the Old Testament allow participation in warfare?" they ask.

3

GOD'S PLAN IN THE OLD TESTAMENT

WE have examined the record of the gospels concerning the teachings of Jesus and His attitudes toward His enemies. We have looked at what Peter and Paul taught. We have seen the writings of the church fathers and the history of the church in the reformation.

It is time to answer the question, "What about war in the Old Testament?" This is a just question, and one that has troubled many Christians.

Between World War I and World War II, I attended a joint meeting of the Evangelical Theological Society and the American Scientific Affiliation. The former is composed of Christian scholars who hold to the full inspiration of the entire Bible, and the latter is made up of devout Christians who are working in the field of science. It was a most interesting meeting. In the course of the discussion, the military threat of Russia to the United States was mentioned. A seminary president commented that the sooner the United States bombed Russia off the face of the map, the better off we would all be.

The next day the moderator read a question which someone had handed him: "How can a Christian call for the total destruction of a people?"

The professor who had made the statement arose. At first he seemed a bit embarrassed or unprepared. He then said something to this effect: "If one studies the New Testament he gets the impression that Christians should simply be suffering witnesses." (I thought, "My! What a fine start!") He then added "But if one reads the whole Bible, he finds out that there is also a place for war."

The professor was, of course, appealing to the Old Testament. Many other people today do the same thing to justify war.

The Old Testament Teachings

Some Bible scholars do not consider the New Testament more binding on the church than the Old Testament. They hold to what might be called a "flat Bible" approach to biblical interpretation. If one considers the Old Testament as equally binding for the church, then the professor's way of thinking is valid. In other words, we may use Old Testament statements to soften the high ethical demands of Christ and the apostles! But this simply is not true. The New Testament holds to a higher standard for human behavior. For example, the Old Testament allowed polygamy, provided the two wives were not blood sisters (Leviticus 18:18). Do Christians therefore take two women as wives, provided they are not sisters? Indeed not.

The Old Testament recognized the office of the avenger of blood. And when the avenger of blood came upon the man who had committed murder, he was to put him to death (Numbers 35:19). Is that rule still in effect?

And capital punishment was not confined to murder in the Old Testament. Anyone who struck his father or his mother was to be put to death (Exodus 21:15). A kidnapper was to be punished by death (Exodus 21:16). Anyone who cursed his father or his mother was to be put to death (Exodus 21:17). A woman guilty of sorcery was to be put to death (Exodus 22:18). A person involved in bestiality was to be put to death (Exodus 22:19). An idolater who sacrificed to any deity other than the Lord was to be utterly destroyed (Exodus 22:20). Even disobedience to father or mother was to be punished by stoning to death (Deuteronomy 21:21). Further, if a family member sought to lead his relatives to worship other deities, he was to be stoned to death, and the persons whom he sought to lead astray were to hurl the first stones (Deuteronomy 13:9, 10)! Shall Christians therefore advocate the same kind of regulations today?

The Old Testament had a simple divorce system. When a man married a wife and found her displeasing in some way, he could give her a written release. She was then free to find another husband. The only restriction was that if a man divorced his wife, and she married another man, he could not marry her again if the second husband died or divorced her (Deuteronomy 24:1-4). Is this the guide for Christian marriages? Indeed not.

Christ Explains the Old Testament

One day the Pharisees called to Jesus' attention lawful grounds for divorcing one's wife. Jesus pointed them to the Original Plan of God for the race. His law was to leave and to cleave: to leave the parents, and to become one with the wife (Genesis 2:24). Divorce was not God's plan.

The Pharisees then brought up the Mosaic command for the husband to write a certificate divorcing his wife. In reply Jesus chose a different verb: Moses did not command divorce, said our Lord; he permitted it. And he permitted it because of the people's hard hearts! The Savior then went on to forbid any and all divorce except where the marriage is broken by unchastity of heart and life. (See Matthew 19:3-12.)

The relation of the church to the Old Testament is a complex matter. Theologians often divide the Old Testament law into three parts: (1) ceremonial law, (2) civil law, and (3) moral law.

Christendom as a whole agrees that the ceremonial law was done away in Christ. This applies to ritual cleansings following the birth of a child, circumcision of boys, and the deaths of family members. Ceremonial laws also included those laws governing clothing, foods, agricultural reguations, animal sacrifices, and the priesthood. It regulated Judaism's religious calendar, including annual festivals, monthly and weekly sabbaths, and the like. The New Testament clearly teaches that the sacrifice of Christ on the cross of Golgotha set Christians free from all these ordinances (Galatians 3—5; Colossians 2:8-23; Hebrews 8:6—10:22).

While it is true that the New Testament never explicitly pronounces the Christians free of the Old Testament civil law, it is obvious that civil law was given to Israel *as a nation*. And it is equally clear that the church is not a nation, for its members are scattered through many nations where they are subject to the laws of their land. Christians shall pray for their rulers, and shall seek to live tranquil and quiet lives there in all piety and holiness (1 Timothy 2:1, 2). There is no way for us to live today under the Jewish rules of the Jewish nation of which we read in the Old Testament.

The moral law of the Old Testament in relation to that taught by Christ and the New Testament involves both continuity and expansion. It is like the relation of a bud to a flower. The bud develops into the flower and the flower shows the end for which the bud was formed.

The basic moral principles of the New Testament are all set forth in the Old Testament. It was Christ Himself who set the pattern for the reading of the law of God, Old Testament and

New. Not only is murder wrong (OT), so is unrestrained anger (Christ: Matthew 5:21-24). Not only is adultery wrong (OT), even looking at the opposite sex to lust is sin (Christ: Matthew 5:27-30). Not only is it wrong to break an oath (OT), even breaking one's word at all is wrong (Christ: Matthew 5:33-37). Not only is personal retaliation wrong (OT), there shall not even be resistance to the evildoer (Christ: Matthew 5:38-42).

Jesus Fulfills the Law

Jesus did not abolish the Old Testament law of God. Rather He fulfilled it. That is, He recognized its divine origin and authority, and made it even sharper than it was under Moses. Jesus showed the true intent and purpose of the law. Therefore, the New Testament defines the real meaning of the law. We also find that every New Testament writer grounds his Christian instruction in the Old Testament (Romans 3:2). The writers of the New Testament books quote or refer to the Old Testament over 2,000 times. Every doctrine in the New Testament is based on the revelation of God in the Holy Scriptures of the Old Testament.

The New Testament writers, following the lead of Christ, built their house of faith on the firm foundation of the Old Testament. But some of the things that were permitted in the era before Christ because of the spiritual immaturity of the people—their "hardness of heart"—are generally not explicitly rejected in the New Testament. They are just passed over.

An example is the status of women. In the Old Testament, women were definitely less responsible than men. When a woman made a vow, if she was unmarried, her father had to confirm it; if married, her husband had to confirm it! (Numbers 30). Only a widow or a divorcee could act independently of some man!

The place of women was vastly higher in Israel than in the surrounding pagan nations. But it was our Lord who treated women as full persons. We had to wait for the New Testament to find women recognized as "co-heirs of the grace of life" (1 Peter 3:7). The high place of women in the Gospels and in the Epistles of the New Testament is a major advance over their Old Testament status. We must face a basic truth concerning the Old Testament: God then permitted certain kinds of behavior that He does not permit in the New Testament.

The New Testament Completes the Old

The Old Testament revelation of God and His will was preparatory and incomplete, while the revelation in Jesus Christ is final, full, and clearly stated. It is therefore dreadfully wrong to push aside the full revelation in Christ to justify sub-Christian behavior by appealing to the things God allowed in Israel only because of their spiritual immaturity.

To say that one must still swear oaths just because God permitted it in the Old Testament is to act as if the Son of God never came down from heaven to teach us the will of God perfectly. To say that a man has the right to divorce his wife because Moses permitted it and to ignore the lasting marriage relationship taught by our Lord, is also dreadfully wrong. To say that a woman cannot make a vow which is binding except if confirmed by a man (father or husband) is to overlook the way Christ lifted woman up to man's side as his "co-heir" of eternal life. And to try to justify warfare because of Israel's numerous wars and to reject all that Christ and the apostles said about nonresistant suffering and forgiving love is equally unsound teaching. Abraham's marriage to several wives does not make polygamy right now, neither do David's wars make it right for Christians to kill in the armed forces. *Our final guide in theology and ethics must be Christ and His Spirit-filled apostles,* the record of which is found in *the books of the New Testament.*

People sometimes ask, How far shall we take the instructions of Jesus to be kind, forgiving, and nonretaliatory? That is not the proper question at all! The real question is, If we take Christ's teachings at all seriously, can we voluntarily participate in warfare at all? Could there possibly be a more total rejection of the words of our Lord than the waging of modern warfare?

4

THE INDIVIDUAL AND PEACE

THE way of peace calls for all-out discipleship. A Christian cannot have worldly goals in life, and follow worldly methods to attain them, and then when war comes suddenly recall that he is not of this world. To follow peace means that the believer is a New Testament Christian by conversion, by consecration, by complete dedication of himself to the cause of the kingdom. Christ wants our total being. He wants the heart and He wants the whole person. Following Christ means that one no longer lives to accumulate wealth, to seek honor and fame, and to enjoy the pleasures of the flesh. A Christian may enter any honorable work (farming, business, teaching, medicine, social work, factory employment, law—the possibilities are endless) but that work dare not engage all of his time and energy. The way of peace that Jesus taught touches every part of life—our personal lives, our family and community life, our work, and the larger society.

People of Peace

William Carey (1761-1834), the father of modern Protestant missions, worked part of his life on an indigo plantation in India. Later he became a professor of Oriental languages in a college in India. The real goal of his life, however, was the extension of the gospel.

George Washington Carver (1864-1943), the son of slaves, became an outstanding scientist and artist. He worked particularly on the peanut and the sweet potato, to see what could be done with the limited crops grown on the poor farms of the South. He gave God the glory for his incredible successes. He felt that his discoveries were really the work of God. He did not patent his discoveries, but shared his findings for all men to profit by them. Although his work was not primarily religious in the narrow sense, he was truly a servant of the Lord. He carried no bitterness. The love of Christ constrained him. Freely he received; freely he gave. In 1935 he became an assistant in the Bureau of Plant Industry of the U.S. Department of Agriculture. He painted as a hobby, and as early as 1916 was highly honored by being elected a Fellow of the Royal Society of Arts (London). It was as a Christian that he tried to raise the level of the poor of the land. He also did more for his race than can be stated in words.

Harold S. Bender (1897-1962) was the son of George L. Bender, longtime treasurer of the Mennonite Board of Missions and its predecessors. George supported himself mostly by working for the post office department. Harold was a very bright youth who likely could have achieved worldly success had he lived for it. Instead, he felt that he was born into the Mennonite Church for a divine purpose. He devoted his great talents to teaching in a small Mennonite College (Goshen), to serving on the executive committee of the Mennonite Central Committee, at times serving as a relief commissioner as well. He was chairman of the Peace Section of the international Mennonite peace committee; president of the Mennonite World Conference, and chief editor of the four-volume *Mennonite Encyclopedia*. A minister and teacher, he was the chief founder of Goshen Biblical Seminary and of Bethany Christian High School. I never knew a man who was concerned so little about money for himself, and who was as creative in raising money for the work of Christ. His contributions toward peace were positive.

In the Home

The home is a common testing ground for the way of peace in everyday life. To practice the way of peace husbands and wives are open with each other. They constantly assure each other of their unique love for each other, daring to discuss and talk through their differences to the best possible resolution of them. They dedicate their home to Christ and the church and work together to raise their children in the way of peace. They do not run to a lawyer for a divorce when they confront a seemingly impossible problem. They pray together, commit the problem to the Lord, and wait for the Lord's solution: all the while strengthening each other in the most holy faith. When they make mistakes, they forgive generously. Their love is thereby enhanced. When their children need discipline, the parents stand together, and any little punishments that need to be given are prompt, in love—never in anger—and are quickly forgotten. Christian parents demonstrate obedience to those "who have rule over them"—in church or state—as long as such rule does not conflict with God's Word.

In such a home, children are intensely aware of the central values for which their parents live, and tend to adopt those same values as they grow up and establish homes of their own. Such a family may live in an Indonesian village, on the plains of Paraguay, or on a small farm in Switzerland. Their way of peace contributes to the program of Christ in all the world.

In One's Community

Those who follow the way of peace seek by much prayer and constant surrender to live in peace and good will with their neighbors. When neighbors express hostile attitudes, we make special effort to show love and forgiveness, in the hope that our neighbors may come to understand the meaning and significance of Christian love. We hear insults with patience and unreasonable demands with a sacrificial spirit.

One of my Christian friends moved next door to a non-Christian in a small town in New Jersey. He had scarcely moved in before the neighbor came to see him.

"Do you know," asked the neighbor, "that the line fence is a whole foot inside my land?"

"No," said the Christian, "I certainly did not know it. Let's get to work and move the fence to the true line."

The non-Christian was utterly unprepared for such a reply. He hesitated briefly, then replied, "Oh, I guess we'll just leave it where it is!"

But suppose they had moved the fence. Which is more important: an extra foot of land along a line fence, or the possibility of winning a person—possibly a whole family—for Christ?

In Colonial America, when church membership was only about 5 to 10 percent of the population, a man of God named Peter Miller (1709-1796) lived at Ephrata, Pennsylvania. He was a member of a branch of the German Baptists (now Church of the Brethren), a Peace Church. Miller was a learned man, a master of many languages, and a humble disciple of Christ. One of his neighbors was in the American army whose Commander-in-Chief was General George Washington, later president of the United States. This neighbor of Miller's was guilty of some misdeed as a soldier and was scheduled for a court-martial to be presided over perhaps by General Washington. The penalty could have been severe.

When Peter Miller learned of this, he trudged sixty miles through the snow to seek an interview with the general. He pleaded eloquently that the general extend mercy to the man in deep trouble. Washington was evidently moved by the plea, and said, "Well, I'll see what I can do for your friend."

The general was likely very surprised when Peter Miller replied simply: "Oh, he is not my friend; he's my worst enemy!"

That is the way of peace!

Full Commitment Required

It appears that if we are to stand for nonresistance, for the way of peace, there is only one way to do it. It takes more than a hatred of war. More than a recognition that people ought to be Christlike. More than a reluctance to shed blood. We must make *the firm decision that under no circumstances, and for no cause, will we take any other position than that of being suffering witnesses of Christ, fully resolved to accept whatever God may allow to come upon us.* This was the decision of Jesus, it is what He taught, it was the position of the apostles, and it is the ethical instruction of the entire New Testament to Christian disciples.

A Costly Way

The way of peace means we may need to "take the wrong" (1 Corinthians 6:7). It may involve martyrdom—it often has. For example, early in 1954 the intensity of Mau Mau terrorism in Kenya was increasing. Three church leaders, who met together for prayer and sharing each morning, were very concerned about what they and their brethren should do. A large number of church members had joined the Mau Mau, taken the oath, and become sympathizers. To many it seemed that there were only two choices—to join the Mau Mau, or to be a traitor by siding with the foreign government. But those who loved Jesus refused to take the Mau Mau oath, carry spears, or kill. They couldn't become a part of the Mau Mau resistance.

The second choice was to side with the government. But since it was putting down resistance with guns and was hunting the Mau Mau in the forest, the brethren said, "We can't do that. The only way we can go to the Mau Mau is with the Bible and with love. We love the terrorists and we love the white men. We don't love the *sin* of the terrorists or the *sin* of the white men. We love and pray for them all. We want to testify to them."

It seemed to the three who were praying that there was a third way. They decided to make the Weithaga station into a Christian camp—a refuge for scattered brothers and sisters around the countryside who were praising God. Some of them very much alone, very vulnerable to the Mau Mau who were killing them one by one. School was not in session at that time, so the school buildings were turned into dormitories. On February 16, 1954, 400 men and women, brothers and sisters, came to Weithaga as a testimony that they were choosing a third way—neither for the Mau Mau nor for the government, but for Jesus Christ. They gathered and prayed. The Lord showed them plainly that it was not for them to fight.

They said, "We do not want to fight the Mau Mau. Our work is to pray for them. If we meet them we may be able to help them by giving them the Word of God. If they hate us, we will not hate them in return. They are our brothers and we love them. As to the white men who are killing our people, we love them and whenever we meet them, it is our duty to warn them and to give them the Word of God. We love our white brothers for they are children of God also.

"What does the sinner need? He needs love. Therefore, love is our only weapon." Someone read the verse, "Not by might, nor by power, but by my spirit, saith the Lord of Hosts." One after another, these nonresisters were killed. When one of them was killed, all gathered together, as if it were a wedding day, and they buried the person, praising Jesus. They kept on praising Jesus, and people were saved.

Some of those who had gathered in the Christian camp were killed. Many were beaten and suffered. But a few years later there was great rejoicing. Many of those who had been fighting, killing, and beating the Christians, turned and themselves were saved. Twenty years later, many are loving Jesus. Some of the men who were in the forest are now evangelists, pastors, and deacons. Some are elders in the church, and they love the Lord. "But if we had had hatred," say the Christians who went through the fire, "if we had had hatred in our hearts and joined with those who were fighting and killing, there would have been a great separation, and the door would not have been open for them to come back to Jesus and to repentance."*

Holding to the position of suffering love and nonresistance is not a position of prudence, of doing what we calculate will be best for us. We rather hold to it because we understand it to be the will of God. We see it practiced, as well as taught, by the Lord Jesus Himself. We understand the New Testament to ask for it. We know that this doctrine of love was also the understanding of the church fathers who lived in the earliest centuries of the Christian church. It is a costly, but proven way.

Objections

As soon as a nonresistant Christian expresses his convictions against war and violence, an uneasy doubt arises in the minds of some opponents: "Do you hold to the basic New Testament principle of salvation by grace through faith?" they ask. The answer, of course, is a resounding "*Yes!*" Mennonites are firmly committed to the great Reformation principle of justification by faith.

Other people become still more uneasy because they have had a son or a father or other relative or friend who died in some war. They ask, "Are you trying to tell me that they went to

*From The Foundation Series story collection, used by permission of The Publishing Council, The Foundation Series.

hell?" The answer is, "By no means are we the judges!" God is the Judge, and He is merciful and compassionate. It is wholly improper for any of us to try to play His role. All of us are saved only by the grace of God.

A third objection comes in the area of international relations. "What should Nation A do if Nation B does this or that act of war?" The nonresistant can but humbly reply that he does not have simple answers to the complex problems faced by the governments of earth. He is rather *concerned to follow the peace principles of his Lord, Jesus Christ, as they are set forth in the New Testament.*

Basic Concepts of Nonresistance

In summary here are the basic concepts of nonresistance:

1. This position of nonresistance assumes the separation of church and state. Nonresistant Christians acknowledge that it is the function of the state to maintain law and order in society by the threat of force. But the nonresistant believes that the function of the church is to teach the Word of God, seeking to win the non-Christians to the Lord, and attempting to build up believers in Christ.

2. Members of the church are regenerated children of God, partakers of the divine nature, earnestly seeking to be faithful disciples of Christ, and ready to accept unjust suffering in meekness and forgiving love.

3. The teachings of Christ are not impossible ideals, but genuine guidelines for regenerated

disciples who walk in the Spirit.

4. In addition to being Divine Savior, Jesus Christ is the Perfect Teacher. Christians seek to follow His style-of-life in the power of the Holy Spirit.

5. The Spirit of God moved those who wrote the books and letters of the New Testament—many of whom Christ had personally taught while on earth. Thus, they left true and trustworthy doctrinal and ethical guidelines for His church.

6. The full revelation of God has come once for all in Christ. Therefore, we no longer set the preparatory and non-final revelation of God in the Old Testament against the teachings of the New Testament.

7. The way of peace is valid, we believe, if it reflects honestly the letter and the spirit of the New Testament writings.

5

SOCIETY AND THE WAY OF PEACE

WE live in a world of much injustice and trouble. American Indians have been pushed off their lands in many cases by means which were truly painful to people of conscience. Even today they are suffering in various ways as a minority people. This seems to be the painful condition of minority groups—whether the Indians of the USA, the Mé of Canada, or the Ainus of Japan. Perhaps every nation has a minority problem in one way or another.

Human slavery has been abolished in most parts of the civilized world. However, racism and the smoldering resentment caused by the injustices of the slave system will long remain. The treatment of men and women in prisons today cries for reform.

Prostitution and the use of habit-forming and mind-altering drugs are widespread social evils often promoted by organized crime.

Corporation officials and their employees frequently manifest cruel and selfish attitudes as each side struggles for as much of the profits as possible.

Meanwhile the crime rate rises: thefts, arson, rape, murders—it is obvious that the Bible knows our need when it describes the sin of the human heart and the need of the new birth, of regeneration by the Spirit of God. Our society—whatever our nationality—is subject to the judgment of God.

The Good News of the Gospel

We cannot bring the masses to regeneration and divine deliverance by tinkering with the structures of society. But we can see them delivered as individuals when we share with them the gospel, and see them by a mighty work of God become new creatures in Christ.

This good news is that there is forgiveness in Christ, new birth in the Spirit, a faith union with Christ which enables the individual to walk in holiness and victory.

A good illustration how the conversion of a man changes his relation to his society is Cyprian, the African church leader. The son of a wealthy Roman officer, Cyprian had much of what the world could give. As a mature man, perhaps in his early forties, Cyprian read the writings of Tertullian and came to greatly admire that man of God. A Christian named Caecilius lived in Cyprian's home and deeply impressed him with the beauty of the Christian life. Finally Cyprian began to study the Holy Scriptures. As a result, he was converted about the year 246 when he was probably in his late forties. He "forsook the world," sold his estates, and became a catechumen—one being instructed in the faith prior to baptism. He was himself ordained as an elder in 247, and the next year was consecrated as a bishop, in which office he served as the head of the North African clergy.

Violence in an Evil World

In a letter to Donatus, Cyprian laments the awful sin of the world. He suggests that Donatus transport himself in imagination to a high mountain and look down with compassion upon the evil world. "Consider the roads blocked by robbers, the seas beset with pirates, and wars scattered all over the earth. The whole world is wet with mutual blood; and murder, which is a crime if done by an individual, is called a virtue when it is committed in war! Freedom from punishment is claimed for the wicked deeds of war, not on the plea that they are guiltless, but because the cruelty is carried out on a grand scale."

Cyprian goes on to lament the awfulness of the games in the arena where men fought and killed to gratify the eyes of the masses. "Training is undergone to acquire the power to murder, and the achievement of murder is its glory." He lamented also the defiling influence of the theaters which fed the minds of people with lust and all manner of sin.

Cyprian confesses that while he was still in darkness he simply could not grasp the possibility of experiencing what he heard called "divine mercy." He did not understand that a person could be born again! Cyprian was deeply aware how sin corrupts human nature, how it binds those who have long lived in it. He simply could not believe in the possibility of becoming a new man, a new creature. But he experienced just that when he turned to Christ, was baptized, and was "animated by the Spirit of holiness."

Cyprian was a man of great influence in the ancient church of North Africa. Unfortunately, he attributed almost magical power to the water of baptism, and exalted the office of bishop almost to the point of making it the center of the life of the church. But he was also a devoted servant of God, a man of a beautiful character, and a true hero in the dreadful empire-wide persecution of the Valerian era. Cyprian died as a true martyr of Christ in the year 258.

The evils of society are just as real now as in the day of Cyprian. War has become infinitely more awful. Today, in many parts of the world, we have TV and films that contain much violence. Yet even today, individual by individual, we, as a part of society, influence it.

Victory Over Violence

The history of victory over a given social evil often goes like this. First, everyone more or less sees the evil as a part of the social order. Second, God raises up a "prophet" who lays the evil on the conscience of God's people, who sooner or later see its evil. Third, the conviction that it is wrong spreads to the larger society and the evil is then eliminated by law.

Slavery is a case in point. The first known protest against slavery in Colonial America was written at Germantown, Pennsylvania (now a part of Philadelphia) in 1688. The basic conviction seems to have come from the Mennonite background, for Mennonites were always opposed to slavery. The four signers of this protest in 1688, however, were then Quakers. (One had been a Mennonite and later returned to the Mennonites; one had been a Lutheran Pietist.) The Quakers of the Monthly Meeting who received the petition passed it on to the Quarterly Meeting. The Quarterly Meeting then passed it on to the Yearly Meeting—but none of these bodies would take a stand against slavery.

The second witness against slavery—the "prophet"—was a godly and sensitive man of God, the Quaker John Woolman (1720-1772) of New Jersey. He began to preach for the Quakers when twenty-one. He also preached to the American Indians. In his famous *Journal*, Woolman lays bare his soul, and we learn how God led him. He would sense God leading him to make a trip somewhere to witness to his brotherhood against the evils of slavery. He would ask his Quaker congregation for counsel. They would test his sense of divine leading, approve it, and then commission him for his journey. In his typically quiet and humble way he would share the conviction of his soul that it was a sin to keep a person in slavery. Sometimes in his *Journal* he admits to having said too much. Other times he felt that he had been a faithful mouthpiece for his God, and his heart was at peace. In 1772 he made a trip to England to give his Christian witness against slavery. But while there he died of smallpox.

The amazing achievement of this quiet witness for Christ was that by the time of his death few slaveholders were left among American Quakers!

Several generations later President Abraham Lincoln issued the famous legal document, the Emancipation Proclamation, effective January 1, 1863, setting all slaves in the United States free. The Mennonite influence and example, which led to the 1688 protest against slavery, and the highly effective conviction of God's servant John Woolman were the beginnings of a drastic change in American Society. Society can be changed by following God's leading.

War remains a major evil of world society. Conviction against war faces a more stubborn resistance than conviction against slavery. However, in this century we have such an imposing panel of witnesses that one wonders what their impact will be. Just to mention a few: Cecil John Cadoux of Great Britain; Roland H. Bainton of Yale University; Culbert G. Rutenber, a Baptist leader; William R. Durland, a Catholic scholar; and Mennonites such as Guy F. Hershberger and John H. Yoder. No large denomination has yet condemned all participation in warfare: only the small bodies such as the Mennonites, the Church of the Brethren, and the Friends cling to their biblical nonresistance—and not all members even of those groups are altogether convinced. At least, the pressures of wartime have succeeded in inducing some members of the Peace Churches to enter the armed forces. But the witness must and will go on. Here and there, individuals are being heard and governments are taking notice of their conviction against war.

Would that God might raise up a few dozen employers who could show the way to avoid the continuing power struggle between the huge corporations and the powerful unions, each fighting for all the money possible. Such Christian employers could take a totally different approach. They would begin by being open with their employees. They would share fully with them their hopes, dreams, failures, and successes and invite their counsel and help. In times of slow business, all employees might be invited to take a smaller salary rather than to lay off the most recent employees. Profit sharing would be a standard procedure. There might be an annual salary with no deductions for periods of illness. If the workers were fully informed, they would no doubt be happy to see the company withhold sizable portions of the income in order to replace out-dated machinery and to make necessary improvements and expansions. The key words here are mutual trust, openness, and cooperation. It is likely that only a Christian group could ever make a success of this kind of a project.

Peace Often means Suffering

Sometimes the only way to overcome violence is through suffering and death. In a village of Uganda lived a chief who did not accept the things of God. A group of boys sang to him everyday. He grew to love them very much. After sometime, the Christian faith came to his country, but the chief was very much against it. He did everything to stop it, and forbade his people to worship Jesus Christ.

But among the singers was a boy named Lwango. He prayed to Jesus; and his friends went with him to worship. Soon all of them became Christians. The chief's son was among them.

Someone told the chief that his son whom he loved very much had become a Christian. The chief warned the boys about a law that if anyone was caught worshiping Jesus, he was to be burned to death. The chief asked Lwango to choose—to leave his faith in Jesus or to be burned. Lwango and the others said, "We'd rather be burned, we are followers of Jesus."

The chief hid his son in his house, and began to burn the singers, one by one. The son came before his father and said, "If you kill them, you will have to kill me. I also am a Christian." There was no way out; the chief killed his own son. All of them died because of their faith in Jesus. They knew that although they died, they had eternal life.*

---

*From The Foundation Series story collection, used by permission of The Publishing Council, The Foundation Series.

The Hutterites, who for centuries have lived in peace and harmony with no individual owning anything, are a challenging example of suffering to overcome violence. The Society of Brothers, founded in Germany in 1920 by Eberhard Arnold, joined with the Hutterites and now practice "living in Christian community." Members own no private property.

The worst clash of the Hutterites in their life in North America in the last hundred years occurred in 1918. Because some local patriots were determined to make these German-speaking Americans support World War I—"to make the world safe for democracy"—several "brothers" were severely mistreated as conscientious objectors to war. This maltreatment was contrary to official government policy and should be regarded as one of the excesses of a nation at war.

David Hofer, Joseph Hofer, Michael Hofer, and Jacob Wipf, four Hutterite young men from the Rockport Bruderhof in South Dakota, were drafted for military service in the spring of 1918. On May 25, 1918, they were put on the train for Lewis, Washington, with many other drafted men. The other draftees were, of course, fascinated and amused by these bearded and strangely dressed "Germans" in their midst. In a rough manner they seized them and gave them "American" haircuts and also removed their beards. The young men wept, for they took this as an omen of worse treatment yet to come.

When they reached camp, they were a trial to the officers. Because of conscience, the four "brothers" refused to sign a promise to obey all military commands. They refused to march. They refused to put on military uniforms. After two months in the camp prison they were court-martialed and sentenced to thirty-seven years in military prison. The commanding general reduced the sentence to twenty years, however. They were then transported under armed guard to Alcatraz, a prison on an island in San Francisco bay. The four young men were chained together, two by two, during the day by handcuffs, but during the night their feet were also fastened.

At Alcatraz their clothes were taken from them by force and they were told to put on the uniforms offered them. They refused to do so. They were then taken to the lower levels of the prison, below sea level, where the cells were quite damp, and put in solitary confinement. The cells were very unclean and the odor was bad. The first 4½ days they received no food, just a half glass of water in twenty-four hours. They had to sleep on the wet, cold cement floor without blankets. For the next day and a half they were chained to iron rods above their heads so that they had to stand. The young men were also beaten. The four were too far apart to converse, but David Hofer once heard Jacob Wipf cry out in German, "O Almighty God!"

After about six days of this abuse, the four Hutterites were brought out into the presence of the other prisoners. One of them, when he saw the shape they were in—all bitten by insects, for example—said with tears, "Isn't it a shame to treat people like that?" That free day they received no food until evening. Then they were once more taken down to their damp cells. There they spent four long and wearisome months, being taken up to the courtyard only for an hour each Sunday under heavy guard.

In late November 1918, in the care of six guards, they were transferred to Fort Leavenworth, the Federal Penitentiary at Kansas City. They were again chained together two by two for the journey of four days and five nights. Arriving at Kansas City at 11:00 p.m., they were noisily driven through the streets at bayonet point. Urged to hurry up the hill to the prison, they arrived there wet with sweat—even the hair on their heads. They were told to take off their outer clothing, so they could put on the prison clothes which would be brought to them. They stood in the cold waiting for the prison clothing until 1:00 a.m. by which time they almost froze. Another wait in the cold came at 5:00 a.m. Joseph and Michael Hofer had to be put into the hospital.

Jacob Wipf and David Hofer were once more put in solitary confinement, chained to bars nine hours a day, fed on bread and water. After fourteen days they ate normally for two weeks, only to go back to bread and water intermitently every two weeks.

Meanwhile Joseph and Michael became critically ill. Jacob Wipf sent a telegram to their wives. The railroad agent in South Dakota hated these "Germans" and lied to the women about where their husbands were. They therefore in error went to Fort Riley.

When the wives finally got the correct information and arrived at Fort Leavenworth, the two young men were so near death they could scarcely speak. By the next morning Joseph had died (November 29, 1918). His wife, Maria, begged to see the body, and was at first refused. In a very determined way she made her way past guards to the commanding officer and pleaded to see her dead husband's body. The officer finally relented. When she was taken to his casket, she saw through her tears that they had clothed him in a uniform! As long as he lived, he had refused a military uniform, but in death the "powers" were victorious.

On December 2 his brother Michael followed Joseph in death. When death came, Michael's wife, his father, and his brother David were present. Shortly before he breathed his last, he raised his weak hands and softly prayed in German, "Come, Lord Jesus! Into Thy hands I commend my spirit." The father pleaded so eloquently not to put a military uniform on the body that the "powers" yielded to his wish.

After the relatives left with Michael's body, David was returned to his chains. The whole next day he stood there in his chains and wept. He could not dry his tears because his hands were chained to the bars.

The following morning David asked a guard if he would please take a message to the commanding officer. In his note David begged that he might be moved closer to his friend Jacob Wipf—so that they at least might be able to see each other even though they were not allowed to converse.

To David's utter amazement, the guard came

back an hour later and told him that he was released! This was more than David could grasp at the time. So the guard took him to the commanding officer, who also assured him that he was indeed released and gave him his papers of release. David stepped through the penitentiary door to freedom. But he just stood there, too paralyzed by fear and confusion to know if it was real. After a while a guard came up to him and asked what he was doing standing there. David said, "I'm not sure whether I have been released or not." The guard told him, "You're released all right, nobody gets out of here unless he has been released."

On December 6, 1918, the Secretary of War issued an order prohibiting the chaining of military prisoners. About five days later, nevertheless, when some Hutterites visited Wipf, he was still in solitary confinement, with his hands chained to the bars for nine hours a day. He was still living on bread and water, but his chains were removed for thirty minutes at noon while he ate.

The visitors took this message from Wipf home to the Hutterite Bruderhof: "Sometimes I envy the three who have already been delivered from their pain. Then I think, Why is the hand of the Lord so heavy upon me? . . . Why must only I continue to suffer? But then there is joy too so that I could weep for joy when I think that the Lord considers me worthy to suffer a little for His sake. And I have to confess that compared with our previous experiences life here is like a palace." He was still sleeping on the cement floor, but was now given four blankets. After December 12 he was no longer chained and some planks were put on the floor for him to sleep on. So many letters were received in behalf of the military prisoners that after Christmas their fortunes improved still more.

On January 27, 1919, the Secretary of War ordered the release of 113 conscientious objectors from Fort Leavenworth prison. It was April 13, 1919, before Wipf was allowed to return home to his Hutterite congregation and his loved ones. He and his brothers overcame violence with suffering.

Different Beliefs

Many of those who favor participation in the military would agree that war is distasteful. Yet they seem to assume that we cannot refuse to fight when our national security is in danger. In private life we should of course be kind and agreeable and forgiving, they say, but we must do a citizen's duty in wartime.

The nonresistant has trouble with this way of thinking. He looks at the subject from a different perspective. He asks what kind of a person a Christian should be, and then tries to face the issues as a Christian.

A story from the Middle Ages will perhaps illustrate the position of the nonresistant Christian. A peasant was strolling one Lord's Day over the land he tilled, and to his astonishment came upon his bishop who was an honorable man, but of all things the bishop was hunting rabbits.

The peasant ventured to remark, "I am surprised that your excellency would go hunting on Sunday."

"I am not hunting as a bishop," was the reply: "I am hunting as a prince."

The peasant scratched his head and answered, "If the devil gets the prince, what will happen to the bishop?"

The nonresistant believes that he simply cannot do as a citizen that which would be sin for him as a Christian.

In World War II, Great Britain had her back to the wall and was literally fighting for her life as a nation. And yet she was so gracious as to give total exemption to those nonresistants who felt that they could not take human life, even in a defensive war. In the United States representatives of the three major Peace Churches and other Christians concerned for the recognition of conscience had a number of meetings with the president of the United States. Perhaps the most important of these meetings was held on January 10, 1940. As Harold S. Bender recalled, the group made the following requests of President Franklin D. Roosevelt:

1. Please do not take the nation down the road of war which has ruined so many European nations.
2. We hope that you will see fit not to adopt universal military training for the United States.
3. If you do nevertheless set up universal military training, please make provision for an alternate peace service for those who because of religious convictions are against war and cannot serve in the armed forces.
4. Will you please see that the official statements

of the Peace Churches on the matter of participation in the military be placed in the Archives of the United States government?

The president said Yes to No. 4, and he promised to do what he could on No. 3. He also courteously inquired how the Mennonite refugees were doing in Paraguay. He was told that they are getting along well without a jail and without an army. He laughed, and said that if the United States could do that we could balance the budget! The president also seemed to be favorably impressed with a positive program for the nonresistants. He was glad, he said, that this had been worked out. "That's getting down to a practical basis. It shows us what work the conscientious objectors can do without fighting. Excellent! Excellent!" The president also suggested that the group lay their plan before the attorney general of the nation.

The outcome of these several contacts, and of many other avenues of witness, was that the Burke-Wadsworth Law of 1940 granted conscientious objectors in the United States the legal right to do work of national importance under civilian direction.

In 1947 Minister P. J. Malagar of the India Mennonite Church and J. N. Kaufman, a missionary serving in India, were chosen to present the concerns of the Mennonites to the committee of four who were preparing a constitution for India. Three of the four replied. One simply acknowledged receiving the statement. A second added: "I do not think that in independent India conscientious objectors will be compelled to do military service." The Honorable Mohandas K. Gandhi, himself opposed to war and violence, replied:

N [ew] D [elhi] 30 6 47

Dear Friend

Your letter [received]. Why worry! I am in the same boat with you.

Yours sincerely,
M K Gandhi

One by one many of the nations of the earth are taking an understanding attitude toward law-abiding citizens who object to war for conscience' sake. Great Britain led the way, followed by Canada, Mexico, West Germany, France, the Netherlands, Italy, and others. May God hasten the day of which the prophets of old sang:

> [God] will judge between the nations
> and will settle disputes for many peoples.
> They will beat their swords into plowshares
> and their spears into pruning hooks.
> Nation will not take up sword against nation,
> nor will they train for war anymore (Isaiah 2:4, NIV).

6

FOUNDATIONS OF PEACE: A SUMMARY

WE have examined what the Scriptures of the Old Testament and the New Testament have to say about peace. We have considered the teaching of Christ, His supreme example, and the teaching and example of His early followers. We have traced the decline of the doctrine of peace and have noted its present status in the church at large.

Of particular interest, is the history of Anabaptist witness and the role of the nonresistant Christian in society today. We will summarize the case for the way of peace in eight concise statements.

Building Blocks to Peace

1. Christians who embrace biblical nonresistance assume that a sovereign God of love is in control of the destinies of men and of nations. Since He knows all things, *He knows who can best glorify Him and advance His cause by death, and who by life.*

About AD 200 the venerable Tertullian remarked that the blood of the martyrs is the seed of the church. The Swiss Reformer Zwingli stated: "Born in blood, the church can be restored in no other way than by blood." In other words, the Christian way to advance the cause of Christ is by being ready to suffer and die. The world wins its battles by killing, Christ and His people seem to have to win theirs by dying. Jesus sends us out as lambs in the midst of wolves (Luke 10:3).

Christians do not, of course, claim to understand the providence of God. That is so far beyond our human comprehension that we do not even try to grasp it. Why did the Lord allow James to be killed with the sword and then spare Peter? (Acts 12). Why did He allow the Auca Indians to slay the five missionaries some years ago? Why are other missionaries, in equally dangerous situations, spared?

We must leave matters of this type to our gracious and all-wise God. We are confident that God knows what He is doing, He is in control, and what He allows to come to pass we will seek to accept with a yielded will.

2. Christians who believe in biblical nonresistance hold that upon becoming a Christian,

each convert is divinely called "to take up his cross and follow Christ." The cross, in this case, is a symbol to him that as Christ chose the cross in His suffering and death, so he will faithfully follow Christ, even unto death for His sake, if need be.

The Apostle Peter told his readers not to be surprised at the fiery trial through which they were passing. Rather, he said, rejoice that you are sharing the sufferings of Christ. And if you are reproached because of the name of Christ, you are blessed because the Spirit of glory and of God rests upon you. . . . If you are suffering as a Christian do not be ashamed, but praise God that you bear that name (1 Peter 4:12-16).

3. Christians who practice biblical nonresistance believe that since the Lord commanded them to *love* the brethren, they therefore *find it impossible to kill Christians in peacetime or in wartime*. George Bernard Shaw, the playwright, in one of his plays describes vividly the hand-to-hand struggle of two soldiers in mortal combat. One was older and one was younger. The older man, as an experienced soldier did well. But the younger, a bit stronger, did slightly better. From time to time as they fought, the young man would catch a glimpse of the face of his opponent which seemed familiar, yet he had no time to figure out who the man was. Finally the young man dealt a death blow to his opponent and he fell and died. And then for the first time the young man saw whom he had killed. It was his own father! So it is with Christian brothers in combat with a Christian brother.

As we saw earlier in 1 John, living by love is a test of being a child of God. The people of God are scattered through the several nations of the earth. Can we therefore put loyalty to our nation above loyalty to the people of God? Can I as a citizen of Austria or of Zaire put my loyalty to my nation above my loyalty to Christ and His church? Nonresistants think that W. A. Dunkerly (1852-1951) put it well, when he wrote under the penname of John Oxenham:

In Christ there is no East or West,
  In Him no South or North;
But one great fellowship of love
  Throughout the whole wide earth.

In Him shall true hearts everywhere
  Their high communion find;
His service is the golden cord
  Close binding all mankind.

Join hands, then, brothers of the faith,
  Whate'er your race may be.
Who serves my Father as a son
  Is surely kin to me.

4. Christians who are nonresistant believe that Jesus defined the relation of Christians to the non-Christian world when He commissioned His disciples. He told them to go into all the world and to make disciples of all the nations, baptizing them and teaching them. They therefore ask: How can ambassadors for Christ *lay aside the Lord's Commission to evangelize* in order to accept an *earthly government's commission to kill*

the soldiers of the hostile nation in modern warfare? This means killing civilians, men, women, the aged, and children as well. Before Constantine the Great, in the fourth century, Christians said they could not do it. They could not do evil. They could not kill, because they were Christians.

5. Biblical nonresistants believe that it is the calling of the Christian to be ready to submit to death oneself and to allow one's loved ones to be killed—*should God so permit*—rather than to destroy the evildoers. In the flesh, this position is not easy; it is likely impossible! But this is the conclusion they come to as they read the inspired gospels and epistles of the New Testament. Most nonresistants would, of course, take whatever measures they could, short of killing the criminal, to avert the injury or death of their loved ones.

6. Biblical nonresistants accept the clear teaching of the New Testament that *government is a divine institution* and that as Christians they owe their government *submission, honor, taxes, and intercessory prayer* (Matthew 22:15-22; Mark 12:13-17; Luke 20:20-26; Romans 13:1-7; 1 Timothy 2:1). Christians are therefore not anarchists. They do not take an arrogant attitude toward the governing authorities.

The question may legitimately be raised, "In what sense is government ordained of God?" The late scholar Edward Yoder (1893-1945), my beloved teacher, held that government is ordained of God in the same sense as marriage. God does not approve of every marriage that is contracted, nor does He approve of all the behavior of every couple. And so it is with government. God does not approve of a man killing off his rivals in order to seize the reins of government. Nor does God necessarily approve of all that a given ruler does.

Even a king himself cannot break the holy law of God without punishment. King David is accounted a good king and established the kingdom of Israel. He, at his best, was a man "after God's own heart" (1 Samuel 13:14; Acts 13:22). Yet when David fell into adultery, and arranged for Uriah's death, we read in Scripture that what David had done "*displeased the Lord*" (2 Samuel 11:27). Again, though it cost him his life, John the Baptist, as a true prophet of God, went in to King Herod Antipas and rebuked him for his sin of living with Herodias, his half brother Philip's wife (Mark 6:18).

The *institution* of government, as the *institution* of marriage, is God-ordained. Regardless of the character of the ruler, Christians shall be submissive. When Paul wrote in Romans 13 to obey one's rulers, the emperor was Nero. Although he had not, to be sure, started to persecute the Christians at that point, he was an exceedingly cruel ruler. Revelation 13 describes the saints of God as undergoing severe persecution, but there is no suggestion that they shall raise an army and try to overthrow the government. Rather, the believers are encouraged to endurance and faith, or faithfulness (Revelation 13:10).

7. Biblical nonresistants believe that although the church shall witness to all men, high and low, yet its prophetic ministry does *not include*

instructions to the government on how it shall most effectively do its work. The church does not, for example, give counsel on the operation of the police force or deal with pirates on the high seas or with criminals who are yet minors. Church and State are two separate institutions and necessarily employ differing means in the fulfillment of their unique functions.

Nonresistants do not have smug and neat solutions for all the complex questions of internal tensions and international relations. For that reason they need to be humble.

Men of God may, however, properly warn rulers against such arrogance as the ambition to rule the whole world. They may protest cruel and inhuman punishments, such as those of political prisoners. They should protest if the government denies religious tolerance and begins to favor one religious faith and to persecute another. They must both protest and disobey any state orders against worshiping and serving the God and Father of our Lord Jesus Christ.

8. Finally, biblical nonresistants owe a great debt of gratitude to the many governments which now recognize the sovereignty of a man's conscience before God and therefore allow Christians to do civilian service for their country instead of compelling them to join its military forces. Martin Luther in his defense at the Parliament of Worms gives us a good example of insisting on the sovereign authority of conscience: "My conscience is captive to the Word of God, and I cannot and will not revoke anything. God help me. Amen."

FOR FURTHER STUDY

Wilbur J. Bender. *Nonresistance in Colonial Pennsylvania*, Mennonite Publishing House, Scottdale, Pa., 1934.

Melvin Gingerich. *Service for Peace. A History of Mennonite Civilian Public Service*, Mennonite Central Committee, Akron, Pa., 1949.

Guy F. Hershberger. *War, Peace, and Nonresistance*, Herald Press, Scottdale, Pa., 1969.

John Horsch. *The Principle of Nonresistance*, Mennonite Publishing House, Scottdale, Pa., 1951.

Culbert G. Rutenber. *The Dagger and the Cross*, Fellowship Publications, N.Y., 1950.

S. F. Sanger and D. Hays. *The Olive Branch, [Nonresistance] During the Civil War*, 1861-1865, Brethren Publishing House, Elgin, Ill., 1907.

E. J. Swalm. *Nonresistance Under Test*, E. V. Publishing House, Nappanee, Ind., 1938.

John A. Toews. *True Nonresistance Through Christ*, Mennonite Brethren, Winnipeg, 1955.

J. C. Wenger. *Pacifism and Nonresistance*, Herald Press, 1968.

John H. Yoder. *The Original Revolution*, Herald Press, 1971.

____________. *The Politics of Jesus*, Eerdmans Grand Rapids, Mich., 1972.

J. C. Wenger is professor of Historical Theology in Goshen Biblical Seminary, a school of the Associated Mennonite Biblical Seminaries, Elkhart, Indiana. He has made a lifelong study of Anabaptism and has published numerous articles and books in the field.

He studied at Eastern Mennonite and Goshen colleges (BA), at Westminster and Princeton Theological seminaries and at the universities of Basel, Chicago, Michigan (MA in Philosophy), and Zurich (ThD).

He has taught at Eastern Mennonite and at Union Biblical (India) seminaries, and has served on the Committee on Bible Translation which prepared the *New International Bible*.

He is a member of the Evangelical Theological Society. He has served on the editorial boards of the *Mennonite Quarterly Review*, of *Studies in Anabaptist and Mennonite History*, and of the *Mennonite Encyclopedia*, and on the executive council of the Institute of Mennonite Studies.

He has served the Mennonites as a deacon, a minister, and a bishop. He has been a member of their Historical Committee, Publication Board, Board of Education, district and general conference executive committees, and of the Presidium of the Mennonite World Conference.

He married the former Ruth D. Detweiler, RN, in 1937. They are the parents of two sons and two daughters.

A familiar sight in his home city of Goshen is J. C. riding his bicycle on a local errand.

www.ingramcontent.com/pod-product-compliance
Lightning Source LLC
LaVergne TN
LVHW020658100826
845148LV00012B/2553

* 9 7 8 1 6 0 6 0 8 9 5 3 8 *